Drink Nature

POETRY MEDITATIONS ON NATURE

KaZ Akers

Cyberwit.net

HIG 45 Kaushambi Kunj, Kalindipuram
Allahabad - 211011 (U.P.) India
http://www.cyberwit.net
Tel: +(91) 9415091004
E-mail: info@cyberwit.net

Printed at VCORE COONECT.

Dedication

To our dog, Chiro, who was loved by so many.

The inspiration for this book.

His love, his smile, his intuitive and healing nature made him a magical creature.

The world needs to know his name and his nature.

He never met a cat he didn't like.

To all the animal family I have loved and lost. You make my world go 'round.

Acknowledgements

My son, Jack Akers-Brownlee, for the design of another beautiful book cover and for inspiring me to leave the world a better place for him and the generations to follow.

My husband, Todd, who puts up with late night writing, and me stopping in my tracks every time I get inspired, no matter where I am. He never laughs at me or rolls his eyes when I put yet another spider, or lizard back outside after they sneak into our home.

To my publisher, Cyberwit, for continuing to support my poetry writing and the poetry writing of so many others.

To all my friends and family who are a constant source of love and support, no matter what direction my writing takes, and who never chide me for being "too sensitive".

Preface

Of all the things I have depended on throughout my life, it's nature.

I hope it has known it can depend on me.

I have not always been the best steward.

I have taken advantage.

I have taken nature for granted.

I can remember as a child how much I loved the smell of grass, the air when it rains, climbing trees, and swimming in the ocean.

I make an effort every day to be better to nature. I know I can make a better effort.

It has given me so much that I will never be able to repay.

Nature has never abandoned me. It has always been my friend and companion.

It has scared me, delighted me, and educated me.

I have an insatiable curiosity about nature and it continues to satisfy and peak that curiosity.

I know we can all do more for nature. Let's try.

Contents

The Dog Who Knew All

He nestled tightly up
into the curve of my side.
Instinctively,
intuitively knowing
exactly what to do.
His long, slow deep breathing
pacing my own,
then matching my own.
As if to say:
"I know you're hurting,
that's why I'm here."
His deep and round brown eyes
looked directly into mine.
Bright and glistening
like the surface
of a lake at dawn.
He leaned in
and ever so delicately
licked my cheek.
Never leaving my side
for hours,
for days.
Knowing the exact moment
I began to feel better
his job was done.
He hopped down
and tiptoed away.
Never looking back.
Just gently and peacefully
moving forward with life.

R.I.P. Chiro

Caterwauling

Long, yellow toes
wrap 'round the branch.
Meeting heel to toe
in complete circles.

Talons gripping.
Standing perfectly balanced
on emerald legs.

Waiting.

Neck outstretched
then tucked into its body.
Then outstretched again.

Wings unfurl an astounding width
absorbing the sun's heat.

With a sixth sense for danger
catapulting from the limb
in the blink of a breath.

Caterwauling as it retreats.
Making it abundantly clear
that distance is comfort.

In The Garden

When I can manage to rise with the sun
I sit in the garden
and watch the purslane and hibiscus
in their morning flower.
Each day the hibiscus
looks different.
It behaves differently.
Today its flowers burst skyward,
bathing in the morning heat and dampness.
Tomorrow it will swirl into itself.
Followed the next day by
dropping onto the ground
for the tiniest of lizards to hide.
The purslane withdraws
in the evening
and welcomes the morning
with a jubilant blossom.
If you turn your gaze
you miss it.
Daily the hanging purslane
proceeds to creep.
Outstretching it's vines
like open hands
reaching towards the earth.
Entertaining daily
with a new performance.
A new creation.
How fortunate to be
an enthralled witness
to it all.

Keep Your Mind Gentle

Keep your mind gentle.
If not,
poison will spread
through your veins
and ooze from your pores
undetected until the acid
singes your sinews.

Keep your mind gentle,
lest pain seep into your muscles
like molten lava.
Lest stiffness in your joints
stoop your back
and dull the luster in your eyes.

Keep your mind gentle,
or words shall falter
between your mind
and your lips.

Keep your mind gentle,
like summer breezes,
gentle,
like the Anhinga bird.

Keep your mind gentle.

Nature Accepts You

The trees,
the birds,
the winds
accept you for who you are.
Accept you no matter what state you're in.
If there is pain,
if there is joy,
if there is apathy,
nature embraces you unconditionally.
The wind does not cease to blow.
The sun does not cease to shine.
The birds do not cease to sing and serenade.
Grass continues to grow soft under your feet.
Plants flower.
Ants scurry up and into their hill.
The tide continues to release and absorb,
release and absorb.
As you walk in nature
you're not judged,
criticized,
or ridiculed.
Take nature not for granted.
It has never taken you for granted.
It loves you without care for
your size,
your shape,
color,
or culture.

Move about in nature to know
what it truly means to be free.
No matter what state you're in
nature accepts you for who you are.

  Drink Nature

More Tea?

I am just like you.
Wondering where the time goes
and what happens next.

In the back garden
a lizard jumps limb to limb.
Hibiscus shudder.

Who knows what's in store?
I'm just sipping hot green tea
in the damp night air.

A dog bleats next door
commenting on the road noise.
Shall we have more tea?

Peck, Peck, Pecking

Peck, peck, pecking
on the tall dirt mound facing our home.
Twenty-three pigeons scavenge methodically for food.
More are scattered along the incline of the mound.
Some content to remain at the base.
Peck, peck, pecking.
From my window new construction obscures the valley view,
soon to obliterate it altogether with new homes.
The pigeons fly past my window
and will be gone along with my vista
of the valley and mountains.
Nature and progress are often incompatible.
For a while I will mourn the birds,
their peck, peck, pecking,
and my three dimensional window-framed view
that stretches on for miles.
The pigeons will discover another place for
peck, peck, pecking,
and I must discover another view
from another window.

Rain

Caught in spring rain
without Wellingtons,
without an umbrella,
without a raincoat.
Rain on my face.
Rain on my clothes.
Rain-soaked hair.

The smell of the grasses,
the glistening of the leaves,
bends my mind.
Lizards scurry to hide,
only to reemerge
when the sun appears.

The wind that precedes the rain
coaxes swiftly moving clouds
as they change from
white to grey,
to the darkest of steel.

Mesmerized
into a trance-like state
I observe palm fronds sway,
then dip and bend in the breeze.
Invisible gusts shudder the branches.

Butterfly palms brush the sand
back and forth,

back and forth
tracing wispy, feather-like patterns.

Raindrops imprint
tiny circles in the sand
and nurture the flowers,
trees, bushes and grasses
into full bloom and blossom.

Sunrise

Many years, much time,
friendship lives and does survive,
sunsets and sunrise.

Walking in the Forest

My wish is that you could
at this very moment
experience the scent of the trees.
Reminiscent of great grandmother's cedar chest.
So fresh I never want to leave this prehistoric woodland.
Nonetheless, mosquitoes force me to trudge along
attempting to outrun them.
Sparrows bolt across the trail ignoring me.
Ferns are plentiful and prodigious.
I fear I'm lost walking in the forest,
but little flags assure me
I remain on the right path.
My unreliable internal compass searches for more landmarks.
Needless to say, nothing distinguishes itself.
I hurry in the opposite direction,
kicking up dust and dirt,
confident retracing my steps will end me at start.
The sun sinks past the tree line.
There is no wind.
No birds singing.
Frog croak and crickets chirp
as night falls.
I quicken my pace
and burst through the trees into a clearing.
Hands on knees,
breathing rapidly,
grateful I was never
truly lost.

Drink Nature

Lightning

In the garden pulling weeds.
Long overdue.
Focused,
intense,
but all the same,
fluid.
Crouching left, leaning right.
Balancing on my knees
from weed to weed.
So natural, effortless.
Pulling and tugging,
coaxing and extracting.
The spines on the cacti
and the barbs on the invading plants
fail to pierce my skin.
Clouds gathering overhead.
Thunder in the distance.
As I removed the twisted vine choking the hibiscus
I felt lightning in my head,
in my brain.
A voice said:
"Run!"
Like a startled deer
I jumped up from my kneeling position
and was instantaneously on the patio.
The sliding glass door opened without forethought
and I leapt into my home.
The clouds gathered over the house.

Thunder!
Lightning!
I was safe.
Safe because I listened to the lightning.

Nothing Is Like You

Will you be hard or soft,
sharp or smooth
as I move through you?
Will you sustain
or end my life?
May I count on you
to give me
what I need,
but not too much
as you carve and shape?
When you are loud
I shall plug my ears.
Then when you are peaceful
I shall be carried by you
and drift off to sleep.
Days I will ride you.
Days you will push me.
I can see right through you.
However,
I can never see all of you.
Pungent.
Pure.
Putrid.
Pristine.
Never the same twice,
or thrice.
Uncontrollable,
but in the same breath
you can be transformed.

Nothing,
nothing
is like you…

Water.

Alligator

Every week I take a walk
to stare down the jaws
of an alligator.
Not because I'm fool-hearty.
Not because it's risky,
but because I desire to observe
this ancient being
in its home.
In those moments
to fully realize
I am no longer
the apex predator.
To discover what it feels like
to be vulnerable.
To watch in awe
the power and survival
of age-old beings.
To witness strength
and instinct.

It barely notices me.
Blue black skin glistening in the sun.
One lid opens
to reveal an amber eye.
The triangular head rests in the water
while it's rotund body
languishes in the grass.
Belly full of the morning meal.
Rarely moving a muscle

except to open its gaping jaw
to yawn.
Or stretch a forearm.
Getting even more comfortable
in its marshy, wetlands home.

Green Leaves

Green leaves wail from trees.
Simply cracks in the pavement
of a blue sky.

 Drink Nature

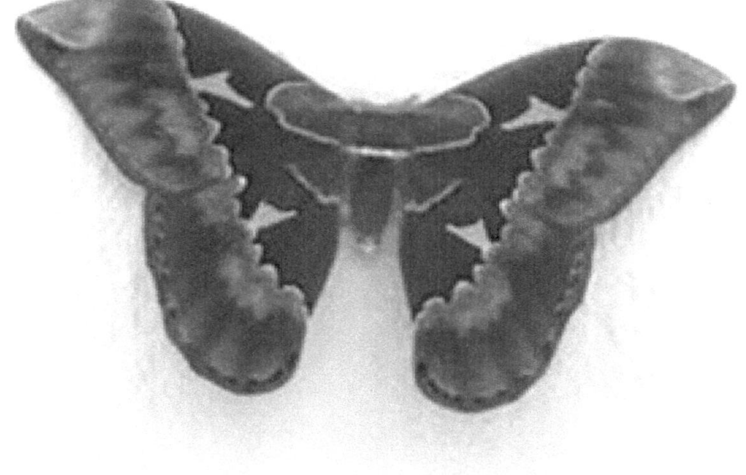

What A Morning!

One,
two,
now three,
and four cottontails bounce.
Going about their business.
Not caring if I quietly interlope
on their morning breakfast.
Small, large,
and may I say,
adorable?
What a morning!
Creatures reveal themselves to me
unabashedly unafraid.
To see and experience such marvels
alive around me
stops me in my tracks;
insisting I understand gratitude…completely.
What a morning!
Forcing me to pause,
take a deep breath,
inhale the honeysuckle,
and suspend myself in these moments of time.
A lucky, lucky gal am I.
What a morning!

Nature Doesn't Give a Damn

Nature does not give a damn
about you.
But you must give a damn
about it.
If you do not water it,
it will still grow.
If you do not feed it,
it will continue to blossom.
Build over it.
Build under it.
Cover it.
Bury it.
Nature will take it back.
Brick by brick,
building by road,
railway and home
nature will consume
and devour.
Rather than accepting you
nature will go on
in spite of you.
and without you.
Be nature's steward.
Let it grow because of you
and with you.

Deer Make Their Way

In the dusk-like morning hours
deer clip clomped
around the perimeter of the house.

The cement sidewalk echoed
with the sound of
hooves of resident deer.

Deer who casually help themselves
to succulent flowers and leaves
that dot the property.

Fences are not deterrents.
Deer make their way.
Discovering the weaknesses
and openings.

Skillfully enlarging small holes
into easy passageways.
Deer-proof has no meaning.

This gives way to plantings
with no deer appeal.
Trees, bushes and flowers
that do not beckon and intoxicate
ubiquitous dwellers
on an island nestled in the sound.

Mother and baby
claim a patch of meadow
on our two and a half acres,
and make it their own.

There is no threat.
No predator to interrupt
or pursue them
during their daily feast.

Drink Nature

Scents

If only we could photograph…
Scents.
The wafting waves of honeysuckle.
The floating fragrance of jasmine.
The rose.
The cherry blossom.
The orange blossom.
And, lest we forget,
the aroma of fresh herbs:
rosemary,
lemon balm
and lavender.
The silent and unseen mists.
Seducing us
into the ecstasy
of what nature provides.
Day by day.
Moment by moment.
What exquisite photographs they would be.
Intoxication for all the senses.

Maryland Morning

Nature out in full force
on this warm and humid day.
A cooling breeze, and a cloudy sky.
Animals scurry,
scamper,
hop,
jump and leap
in every direction.
Certainly, I have never seen so many birds:
the cardinal,
the robin redbreast,
the starling,
the hawk,
crow,
raven,
bluejay,
and sparrow.
I pause for the doe,
the cottontail
and the squirrel.
I linger in the woods
to get another loving glimpse,
on this Maryland morning.

Poet's Note: Dada combats traditional ways of thinking and creating. It is expressed in music, writing, sculpture, painting, photography, puppetry, and more. Dada came into being around 1914 as a protest against the first world war, and is attributed to Tristan Tzara and Hugo Ball, among others. It was influenced by Cubism, Expressionism and Futurism. What appear to be nonsensical words and phrases are up for interpretation and are best read aloud. For me, there is no attachment in Dada and Dada composition is pure artistic freedom. Spontaneity and absurdity are encouraged. Dada's resurgence can me heard in the music of Cirque du Soleil and from David Byrne and Talking Heads.

Nature Dada

Blurp
Blub blub blub blup
Blurp
Blub blub blub blup

Shhhh
Shhhhhhhh
Shhhh
Shhhhhhhh

Bah-ahk, bah-ahk
Ee, ee, ee, ee
Bah ahk, bah-ahk

Blub lub, lub, lub
Blup
Blub lub, lub, lub
Blub blub blub blub

HOH, Hoooooh
HOH, Hoooooh
HOH, Hoooooh

Eeeeeee, ee, ee
Eeeeeeeeee ee, ee

HOH, Hoooooh
HOH, Hoooooh
HOH, Hoooooh

Bah-AHK, bah-AHK!
Bah AHK, bah-AHK!

SHHHHHHHHHHHHHH
Shhhhhhhhhhhh
Shhhhhh

Hawk

Red-tail hawk screeches

high above me

signalling the hunt.

Dappled wings outstretched.

Gliding and hovering

above the crest of the trees;

its presence piercing

a limitless domain.

Will The Birds Sing?

Seeming to wallow
in a stream of deep despair.
Will the birds still sing?

Out Of Harm's Way

I plopped myself from the bow of the sailboat
into the Atlantic ocean outside of Key Largo.
With fins, a mask and snorkel
I glided underneath the surface of the water.
Surrounded by a school of silvery squid,
queen triggerfish,
parrotfish,
angelfish
damselfish
and clear azure blue water
as far as I could see.
No fear,
no apprehension,
just freedom.
My head bobbed above the water.
I glanced in the direction of the sailboat,
squealed with joy, and waved.
My companions casually waved
encouraging me back to the boat.
Not ready to vacate the warm waters,
enveloped by my own bubbles
and bubbles of passing fish,
I waved them off.
More schools of winged squid.
Could anything be so magnificent,
so peaceful?
Will I feel so much a part
of anything ever again?
I surfaced once more to insistent requests

to return to the boat.
This time I acquiesced.
Clearing the water's surface
I climbed into the boat.
"Barracuda were following you.
Following your every move.
Your lack of fear prevented them
from investigating further…
or worse."
Fear has its place,
but in those brief moments
my fearlessness
kept me out of harm's way.

Life On A Fence

Every few days
I sprinkle black oil sunflower seeds
under the fan palm.

No other seeds for the flock of doves
who visit my yard.
These particular seeds are a delicacy.

This gilded morning
one dove perched on the fence post.
Just sitting.

A lone, stub-tailed gecko scaled the fence wall,
catching insects unseen to me,
but abundant nonetheless.

It's light, coral-colored tongue darting so quickly.
Catching a glimpse was the briefest of brief.

Once it reached the height of the fence
it paused.
Dove left its perch
and slowly approached Gecko.

Gecko displayed a warning,
its throat dewlap,
a semi-circle of the brightest orange and yellow.

Dove inched closer.
They peered at each other.

Resolved to share the fence;
they sat.
Separated by inches
and species.
Odd neighbors.

Soon Dove jumped off the fence
to procure black oil sunflower seeds.

Gecko lurched forward, sideways,
and upside down after tiny bug morsels.

Life on a fence.

Will You?

If I love you,
will you love me back?
Will you embrace me,
provide for me,
protect me from
storms,
deluges,
and assaults?
Will you share your wisdom,
your courage,
and your might?
Can you listen to me when I speak,
as I attempt to listen to you when you speak,
shout,
moan
and cry?
Tell me what I must do
to keep you safe,
to help you thrive.
What I must do
to keep me safe,
so I may thrive.
Must we go to such extremes
to make a point about what we need?
My weak self thinks I can bend and shape you
to my ends.
I'm doing my best to listen,
but I'm stubborn and selfish,

in the face of supreme generosity.
Mother of Nature will you teach me?

Will you?

Black Snake

Long black rat snake
curled between the leaves of an outstretched branch
jutting over a bridge,
on a creek.
There for all eyes to see,
but none saw.
I turned the corner,
and there at eye level it was,
in all its beauty.
The branch effortlessly held its substantial weight.
Not until I stood and watched
did others notice.
Out came cell phones and cameras
capturing this seemingly oblivious beauty.
It was aware.
It made no gestures as people approached.
One passerby attempted to stroke the tail.
Admonished by his wife:
"Leave the wildlife alone.
Let them live in peace."
I continued my walk around the lake.
Upon my second pass
I noticed it had slithered farther down the branch
towards the ground
away from prying eyes.

A Delightful Encounter

The armadillo barrelled down the sandy path towards me
as if I did not exist.
It's mission was one thing
and one thing only:
grubs,
worms,
insects.
Such delightful little omnivores.
I suspect we became aware of each other
around the same time.
I slowed my pace
and it pointedly continued on.
It appeared fearless,
not careless,
anxious to continue its exploration.
Barely three feet away it halted,
but displayed no aggression.
Focused, it veered off the path to my left,
into a thatch of trees,
brush,
underbrush,
and leaves.
Unalarmed that I continued to watch
with delight and amazement
it scuttered under this branch
and over that palm frond.
Deeper and deeper into the thick
it hustled out of sight.
A delightful encounter of wary,
but harmless, passersby.

Gecko Domain

Gecko bounced up and down atop the face
of the statue known as Noble Treasure.

It displayed its dewlap over and over
in bursts of bright orange and yellow.

Defying gravity as it balanced
on the alabaster cheek.

Gecko then came to rest prone
in the folded arms of a giant.

Surveying the yard
it signalled undisputed command of the territory.
A declaration of domain.

It slid down the billowy sleeve
and paused, head down,
again gesturing with its sunburst dewlap.

Head parallel to the ground, the reptilian contortionist
became as motionless as the statue.

I turned away for a tick
and in that tick
Gecko disappeared without a trace.

Mother Of Nature

Mother Nature will do anything
to stay alive.
Even if it means destruction.
The living, breathing earth
demands attention
via hurricanes,
typhoons,
earthquakes,
fires,
mudslides,
tornadoes, blizzards, avalanches, thunderstorms, sandstorms,
tsunamis.

She demands our attention,
and we are NOT listening.
Not listening or heeding
so many warnings.

Lip service,
bandaids,
fundraisers,
good intentions.

One thing,
even one small
consistent thing,
can and will
ease her pain.

Mother of Nature will do anything,
anything
to stay alive.

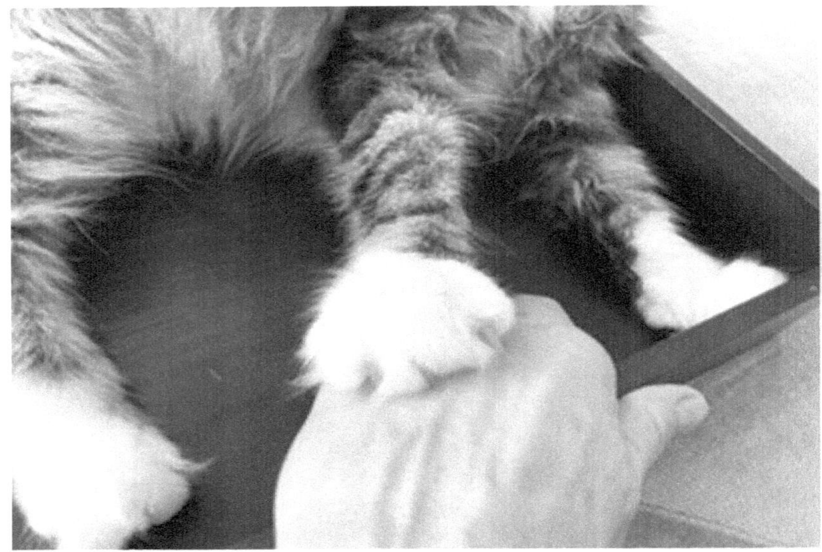

Staring At The Sky

Staring at the sky
time quit counting all the stars.
Life tells the story.